T0220591

Software Testing Automation Tips

50 Things Automation Engineers Should Know

Gennadiy Alpaev

Apress®

Software Testing Automation Tips

Gennadiy Alpaev
Dnipro, Ukraine

ISBN-13 (pbk): 978-1-4842-3161-6   ISBN-13 (electronic): 978-1-4842-3162-3
https://doi.org/10.1007/978-1-4842-3162-3

Library of Congress Control Number: 2017958550

Cover image designed by Freepik

Managing Director: Welmoed Spahr
Editorial Director: Todd Green
Acquisitions Editor: Jonathan Gennick
Development Editor: Laura Berendson
Coordinating Editor: Jill Balzano
Technical Reviewers: Mykola Kolisnyk and Mykhailo Poliarush
Copy Editor: Karen Jameson
Compositor: SPi Global
Indexer: SPi Global
Artist: SPi Global

Distributed to the book trade worldwide by Springer Science+Business Media New York, 233 Spring Street, 6th Floor, New York, NY 10013. Phone 1-800-SPRINGER, fax (201) 348-4505, e-mail orders-ny@springer-sbm.com, or visit www.springeronline.com. Apress Media, LLC is a California LLC and the sole member (owner) is Springer Science + Business Media Finance Inc (SSBM Finance Inc). SSBM Finance Inc is a **Delaware** corporation.

For information on translations, please e-mail rights@apress.com, or visit http://www.apress.com/rights-permissions.

Apress titles may be purchased in bulk for academic, corporate, or promotional use. eBook versions and licenses are also available for most titles. For more information, reference our Print and eBook Bulk Sales web page at http://www.apress.com/bulk-sales.

Any source code or other supplementary material referenced by the author in this book is available to readers on GitHub via the book's product page, located at www.apress.com/9781484231616. For more detailed information, please visit http://www.apress.com/source-code.

Printed on acid-free paper

Contents at a Glance

About the Author ix

About the Technical Reviewers xi

Introduction xiii

▓Chapter 1: Scripting 1

▓Chapter 2: Testing... 21

▓Chapter 3: Environment.. 31

▓Chapter 4: Running, Logging, Verifying 37

▓Chapter 5: Reviewing 43

Index... 49

Contents

About the Author ix

About the Technical Reviewers xi

Introduction xiii

■Chapter 1: Scripting 1

1-1. Do Not Use Record & Play in Real Projects 1

1-2. Do Not Use Pauses 3

1-3. Provide Exit by Timeout for Loops 4

1-4. Do Not Consider Test Automation as Full-Fledged Development 5

1-5. Do Not Write Bulky Code 6

1-6. Verify All Options of Logical Conditions 8

1-7. Use Coding Standards 8

1-8. Use Static Code Analyzers 9

1-9. Add an Element of Randomness to Scripts 10

1-10. Do Not Perform Blind Clicks Against Nonstandard Controls 10

1-11. Learn and Use Standard Libraries 11

1-12. Avoid Copy and Paste 12

1-13. Do Not Use try…catch with an Empty catch Block 13

1-14. Separate Code from Data 14

1-15. Learn How to Debug 15

1-16. Do Not Write Code for the Future 16

1-17. Leave the Code Better Than It Was 17

1-18. Choose a Proper Language for GUI Tests 17

1-19. Remember to Declare and Initialize Variables 18

■**Chapter 2: Testing** **21**

2-1. Do Not Duplicate Tested Application Functionality in the Scripts .. 21

2-2. Each Test Should Be Independent 22

2-3. What Should Not Be Automated? 23

2-4. Ask the Developers for Help 24

2-5. Cloud Testing 26

2-6. Introduce Automation for Corner Cases 26

2-7. The Difference Between Error and Warning 27

2-8. Use the Appropriate Methodologies 27

2-9. Verification of Individual Bugs 28

2-10. Make a Pilot Project Before Writing Real Tests 29

■**Chapter 3: Environment** **31**

3-1. Choose a Proper Set of Tools for Your Needs 31

3-2. Do Not Automatically Register Bugs from Scripts 32

3-3. Do Not Chase After a "Green Build" in the Prejudice of Quality 33

3-4. Learn the Tool You Work With 33

3-5. Make Use of Version Control Systems 34

3-6. Avoid Custom Forms 35

3-7. Simplify Everything You Can 35

3-8. Automate Any Routine 36

■**Chapter 4: Running, Logging, Verifying** **37**

4-1. Run Scripts as Often as Possible 37

4-2. Perform an Automatic Restart of Failed Tests 38

4-3. A Disabled Test Should Be Provided with a Comment 38

4-4. Errors in Logs Should Be Informative 39

4-5. Make a Screenshot in Case of Error 39

4-6. Check the Accuracy of Tests Before Adding Them to the
Regular Run 40

4-7. Avoid Comparing Images 41

■Chapter 5: Reviewing 43

5-1. Write Tests That Even Non-Automation Engineers
Can Understand 43

5-2. Avoid Unneeded Optimization 44

5-3. Review Someone Else's Code Regularly 45

5-4. Participate in Forums and Discussions 46

5-5. Perform Refactoring 47

5-6. Remove Tests That Provide Minimal Benefit 47

Index 49

About the Author

Gennadiy Alpaev has been working as a test automation engineer since 2003. He has worked with many automation tools, including SilkTest, TestComplete, Selenium, and Squish. In 2011 he began to move his expertise toward teaching about testing and automation. Gennadiy has been running online and on-site courses on TestComplete and test automation for independent students and companies ever since. He is a published author, and speaks regularly at conferences on the topic of testing automation.

About the Technical Reviewers

Mykola Kolisnyk has been involved in test automation since 2004 through various activities, including creating test automation solutions from scratch, leading test automation teams, and performing consultancy regarding test automation processes. In his career, he has had experience with different test automation tools, such as Mercury WinRunner, MicroFocus SilkTest, SmartBear TestComplete, Selenium-RC, WebDriver, Appium, SoapUI, BDD frameworks, and many other engines and solutions. Mykola has experience with multiple programming technologies based on Java, C#, Ruby, and more. He has worked for different domain areas, such as health care, mobile, telecom, social networking, business process modeling, performance and talent management, multimedia, e-commerce, and investment banking.

Mykhailo Poliarush is an independent test automation consultant and trainer since 2009, founder of the biggest Russian-speaking test automation community http://automated-testing.info, founder of the test automation consulting company http://sdclabs.com, and his personal website is at http://poliarush.com.

Introduction

After 10 years of working in test automation, I noticed that many things that seem obvious to me are something new and unusual for others. This is quite natural when teaching students, but several times I came across such lack of knowledge among people who successfully worked as automation engineers for 3-4 years. This is explained by the fact that usually on one project testers work with one type of tested application (for example, a web or desktop), while not coming across other types of applications. Similarly, one project is limited to a set of test conditions, automation tools, etc.

Communicating with students and young professionals, I had to return again and again to the same topics. About once a year, I talked about the same thing, every time with new people.

In the end, I decided to formalize them all in the form of a book with a set of tips, which answer the most frequently asked questions and mistakes.

I hope that these tips will help testers involved in automation not to repeat mistakes that have already occurred more than once in our profession, have been repeatedly discussed, and successfully solved.

This book will be useful to those who only step on the path of test automation, as well as those who have experience limited to a small number of projects and automation tools used.

At the same time, experienced automation engineers can find here new or unusual ways of solving problems, even if they have encountered in practice something similar, since each person can approach in his/her own way to the solution of one and the same problem.

CHAPTER 1

Scripting

This chapter describes best practices in automation related to writing code, creating tests, and building your automation framework. Also mentioned are some of the common mistakes that automation engineers produce in their work, and ways to avoid those mistakes. Some tips in this chapter are common for both automation and development, while others are specific for testing automation only.

1-1. Do Not Use Record & Play in Real Projects

Most automation tools (especially commercial ones) have Record & Play functionality: the ability to automatically record certain actions and then play them back just by clicking on the Play button. The seeming simplicity of this functionality is a well-known trap for novice software testers.

Record & Play looks very nice in advertising videos and presentations, but when you actually work, such scripts are not recommended to be used, since they only complicate the process. A recorded script does not use variables, loops, and conditions. Automatic names of created procedures and functions are not usually informative, and all actions are recorded in one function (which can be huge). Very often recorded lines of code are so long that they do not fit on the screen.

Overall, code generated by recording user actions tremendously complicates the support of your tests and their understanding. In the case of a large number of actions, such tests are usually easier to be recorded anew than to be changed even a little bit.

© Gennadiy Alpaev 2017

G. Alpaev, *Software Testing Automation Tips*, https://doi.org/10.1007/978-1-4842-3162-3_1

THE PAIN OF RECORD & PLAY

Once I joined a project where automation of testing was used for several years, but no one took the effort seriously. Tests were recorded, then minimal changes were made (usually code that could not be recorded was added), and afterward tests were run for regression. These tests were very unstable, pauses were used everywhere to somehow stabilize their regular runs, and it was possible to understand these tests only by comments (the testers had to insert comments as the test was recorded; otherwise they could not themselves understand in a few days what this or that line of code was actually doing).

Since the tested application had been developed quite actively, the tests had to be updated regularly. Testers had to spend a week, on average, to make changes to the test suite, which took a few hours to record. One problem was that recording tests anew was also almost impossible, since there were no clear instructions anywhere on what actions and verifications should be performed.

For the next version of the application, the scripts were written manually and what used to take a week was now performed in no more than a day!

A recorded test must be edited and put in order, and it is even better to write the code manually from scratch. The less automatically recorded code is in your tests, the clearer and easier such tests are to maintain.

There are, however, several cases when the Record & Play can be used to good effect:

- When studying a new automation tool, recording is the easiest and most convenient way to get an idea of how the tool works. While you are studying the capabilities of the tool, Record & Play is your best friend.

- If you have a single task and you are sure that you will never need a script later, feel free to use the recording as well.

- For some controls (for example, custom context menus), it can be difficult to get their identifiers and understand how to work with them. In this case, Record & Play will help you to better understand how to work with this control.

In other cases, it is better to use a framework that will help you to create tests faster and more efficiently than recording them automatically.

1-2. Do Not Use Pauses

When you use any application, there are situations when you need to wait for the end of an action, for example, reading data from the database, searching, loading all page elements, etc.

In such cases, a recorded script "doesn't know" that it is necessary to wait and tries to perform further actions, although the application is not ready yet, and the result is a test that fails with errors. Junior automation engineers use a pause in such cases:

```
sleep(5)
```

The wait time in this case is five seconds, and typically the timings are just hardcoded approximations that are based on the current application speed.

Over time, such delays appear everywhere in the tests. And in that proliferation lies the seeds of trouble.

Imagine that at some point the application starts to spend a little more time, and the automation engineer has to make a huge number of hot fixes in a variety of tests. That process is time consuming and error prone. After several similar, mass hot fixes the tester comes to a new solution. He declares a global variable and uses it everywhere:

```
WAIT_TIME = 5
...
sleep(WAIT_TIME)
```

Now we just need to change the delay value in one place so that the wait time is increased everywhere. This approach has one big disadvantage though. If the application starts working faster, our tests will still wait for the same constant time. Since pauses are placed in different places, the total time that the tests work will be much longer than it could be.

The right solution in such cases is to wait for an object or object property. Any action of the application ends with some event: a button that was previously disabled becomes enable (for example, Next button), or a new control appears that was not previously available. Or, on the contrary, some element or window can disappear from the screen (for example, label "Wait for data loading"). Here we have to attach to such events using wait functions. Now the code will look like this:

```
MAX_WAIT_TIME = 5
...
wait_for_object(object_name, timeout=MAX_WAIT_TIME)
```

Function wait_for_object can already be provided by the automation tool, or it will have to be written by you. It checks the existence of the object with a certain interval (for example, once per second) and returns true if the object appeared. If the object does not appear within the time specified by the timeout parameter, the function returns false.

Thus, if the object we are interested in appears in a second, then the wait time will be 1 second. If the object appears after 3 seconds, then the function will work only 3 seconds, etc.

WAITING IS FASTER

Once, when I came to a new project, where automation was used for several years, I found an overall use of pauses. The running time of all tests was at that time several hours. After replacing most of the pauses by waiting for objects, the tests' runtime was reduced by 70%!

Of course, you can't completely abandon the pause. For example, in wait functions such a pause is mandatory. After each verification of the existence of the object, it is necessary to make a small delay; otherwise our script will use too much of CPU time, thereby slowing down the speed of the application under test. As a result, a wait function will look something like this:

```
function wait_for_object(object, timeout)
{
 while(timeout)
  {
   if object.exists()
      return true;
   timeout--;
   sleep(1);
  }
return false;
}
```

Also sometimes there can be situations when an attempt to work with a control immediately after its appearance (or change of its state) leads to incomprehensible errors. In such cases, it is also possible to use small (not more than half a second) delays. For example, in the preceding function you can insert such a delay just before the return true line. However, any pause for a long time is a bad approach when writing tests.

1-3. Provide Exit by Timeout for Loops

Sometimes a test should be continued only after the occurrence of a certain event. For example, we need to wait for a file to be created, so we code as follows:

```
while not file_exists()
{ /* do nothing*/ }
```

If for some reason the file is not created, the script will loop forever, which is clearly not desirable. Therefore, in such situations it is necessary to provide a forced exit by a timeout:

```
timeout = 10;
while not file_exists()
{
  if timeout < 0
  { break; }
  timeout--;
  sleep(1);
}
```

In this example, we decrease the value of the timeout by 1 at each iteration and wait for 1 second. After 10 seconds the value of timeout will be less than 0. As a result, we will exit the loop using the break instruction, thus protecting ourselves from the infinite loop.

In addition, using the sleep instruction, we reduce the load on the processor. Verification will be performed once per second, not thousands of times, as in the first example.

Perform an exit by timeout even in those cases when you are 100% sure that there cannot be a hang-up – because most probably you are wrong.

It makes sense to define similar timeouts in the form of constants at the level of the entire project, and not to set each time anew. For example, you can define two types of timeout: short and long. A short timeout (usually equal to a few seconds) will be used for operations that occur almost immediately, but it is necessary to wait for them to finish: for example, creating a file or deleting a directory, an error message appearance when you enter data incorrectly in a text box, and so on. A long timeout (usually equal to several minutes) is intended to wait for the completion of data loading, the appearance of a window, the response from the server, and so on.

1-4. Do Not Consider Test Automation as Full-Fledged Development

Let us be honest: though automation requires programming skills, nevertheless it is not a full-fledged development project. Automation is usually handled by less skilled programmers, since the work is much simpler and is used for the internal needs of the project.

In 99% of cases, you will not need most design patterns. You will not use transactions when working with databases, the volume of your test data is unlikely to approach the volumes of a real application, and you do not have to worry about the visibility scope of functions. You need general knowledge of object-oriented programming (OOP), the ability to write simple SQL queries, and the ability to run tests in debugging mode.

Therefore, there is no need to try every new approach that you learn about software development in general to the practice of writing automated tests. Do not try to show how smart you are. It is better to show the ability to write simple code that even a beginner will understand (it is quite possible that the beginner will support the tests after you).

Even if your project uses an approach such as behavior-driven development (BDD) or keyword-driven testing (KDT), in which the code is written by one group of people, and the tests are created by another, it is still better to use simpler solutions.

SIMPLE APPROACHES ARE BETTER

One day while writing tests of an installation program, I used several approaches all at once that were new to me. All of my resulting code looked very cool, and was correct from an architecture point of view (when writing tests, I consulted with the project architect and immediately implemented his advices in practice).

After writing all that fancy code, it turned out that the installation programs were not changed for a long time, so there was no need to look at the test code again for a very long time. After a couple of years, the installation programs were changed just a little and I had to look at the old code. It terrified me! I spent several hours just remembering how it worked, and then a few more hours to make the correct changes. My use of fancy techniques years before had come back to haunt me by making my job more difficult.

For the new version of the product, I used the simplest approaches. As a result, the code amount became smaller and the code itself was more understandable.

Of course, there are very complex projects where automation is integrated with development, where the qualification of automation engineers is as high as that of the developers. However, even in these cases, automatic tests are used only for internal needs; they don't impact end users, and they don't need to be written to the same level as the product being tested.

1-5. Do Not Write Bulky Code

Try to follow the rule of "no more than three nested levels" when using conditions and loops in tests. If you need to write code with a lot of nesting, then step back and think about how to rewrite the code differently, for example, to bring a part of it into a separate function, or to make two separate loops or conditions. Complex and confusing code looks beautiful only when you write it, but not when you try to understand how it works.

Here is an example of code that already has one undesirable nested block:

```
for tbl in tables
{
  if table.name == "contacts"
    {
      for col in table.columns
      {
        /*enough nesting*/
```

```
    if col.name == "first"
    {
        /*this block is redundant*/
        print(col.name[0])
    }
    }
    }
}
```

Code with the nesting of more than three blocks is very difficult to debug, especially for a person who did not write it. When debugging such code, it is difficult to keep track of the state of all variables. As a result, searching for a simple problem can take a lot of time.

TOO MUCH NESTING

Once I met a person with whom I worked in one of the previous projects. He was a very smart guy, and he was usually entrusted with complex tasks and he liked to solve them. In a conversation, he boasted to me: "Do you remember those tables that we had everywhere in the application, and each specific table had some features? So I was able to write one big and pretty function that covers all cases, a universal function! There is a 19-level nesting of conditions, can you imagine? I have been writing and debugging it for several months! And no repetition of code!"

No, I could not imagine that, since 19 levels of nesting do not even fit in the editor on the screen in its width. But I can well imagine what it will be like to someone to support such a code after this person leaves. If now there will appear one more table with some other feature, then it will take a few more months to rewrite the existing function (if possible at all).

What this man boasted about is actually a bad programming style. Instead of 1 function with 19 levels, you could write 5 functions with 3-4 levels (one function for each type of table, because among all the variety of tables you could clearly distinguish the similar ones). Doing so would lead to a little duplication of code, but this code could be supported.

Sometimes there is a need for more than triple nesting, but always try to think over possible simpler ways of implementation. One of the options for checking the simplicity of the code is the calculation of the cyclomatic complexity of functions (i.e., the number of independent routes that a function can pass through). For popular programming languages, there are ready-made solutions for such tests.

1-6. Verify All Options of Logical Conditions

When you do verifications in tests with several logical conditions such as the following:

```
if A and B or C
```

be sure to check such code for each condition (A, B, C in this example) and all probable values (true, false).

Quite often programmers overlook "lazy evaluations," resulting in incorrect operation of such expressions. Verify each condition, and you'll catch such problems early.

Also, do not forget to enclose in parentheses those parts of the logical expressions that should be verified together. Do this even if you are 100% sure of the correctness of the computation priority. For example:

```
if (A and B) or (C and D)
```

The presence of parentheses significantly simplifies the understanding of the code in the future. It doesn't matter that you understand the computation priority now. What matters is that the person maintaining the code years into the future understands. Make that person's job easier by clarifying the order with parentheses.

ONLY APPEARING TO WORK

Once, while checking the homework of a student, I paid attention to a complex logical calculation that at first glance shouldn't have worked. Having started the test, I was convinced that the calculation worked fine, but I was very surprised and began to investigate further. It turned out that none of the two parts of the expression worked correctly. It was because of a simple error that the entire expression returned true, and thus the calculation appeared to work when it really did not.

Verify each of your conditions, and avoid getting caught out by subtle errors like the one my student created.

1-7. Use Coding Standards

Beginners usually don't use any rules for the names of variables and functions. They write as they like, completely without thinking about the fact that there may be some rules. Nevertheless, for almost every language there are so-called coding standards, which are recommended to be used.

In big projects such standards become mandatory rules. They must be followed by all programmers, since following standards greatly simplifies the understanding of both their own and others' code.

For many languages, such rules have been developed a long time ago and are generally available. You can take them as a sample and supplement them depending on your internal needs. For example, for variables, you can use different prefixes depending on the type of display object this variable corresponds to.

Let's suppose that you see the following line of code:

```
Main.Search.Click()
```

Obviously, there is a click on the Search object in the Main window, but if there is a Search text box, a Search button, and a Search static text in this window, then you have to guess which object is clicked. Guessing is not ideal.

Let's look at two other examples:

```
Main.btnSearch.Click()
Main.txtSearch.Click()
```

or at these:

```
Main.SearchButton.Click()
Main.SearchField.Click()
```

These examples are much easier to understand. Even without knowing any special rules, everything is clear intuitively. The use of coding standards improves the readability of code, making it easier for you and others to understand it later.

1-8. Use Static Code Analyzers

For popular programming languages, there are special code analyzers that can report the most common errors or inconsistencies in the standards, for example, pylint for Python language, jslint for JavaScript language, etc.

Typical problems pointed to by similar analyzers are too long of functions, noncompliance with naming standards, too many parameters, incorrect indentation, etc. For many popular programming languages and development environments, there are plug-ins that perform these verifications right in the editor while writing the code.

At first, the use of such tools can be difficult, since they show a lot of errors. However, in a few days you will become so used to the tools that you will write code with practically no such mistakes, and the code will become much more readable.

Even better is to force the use of such analyzers when adding code to the repository. To do so, simply write a script that first calls a static code verification, and only if the verification succeeds, perform a commit.

There may be times when you want to prevent certain rules from being checked by an analyzer. Most provide a mechanism for disabling rules, so that you can always disable a particular rule if it suits your project to do so.

1-9. Add an Element of Randomness to Scripts

Imagine that you are testing standard Notepad application. One of the frequent operations that you have to perform will be the operation of opening the file. However, you can perform this operation in several ways:

- select the File|Open menu item;

- press Ctrl-O hotkey;

- press Alt-F-O key combination;

- press Alt (to activate the menu), then several times the down arrow key, then press Enter;

- pass the path to the file as a command-line parameter;

- drag a file to the Notepad window using the mouse.

There are several ways to achieve the same result, but theoretically any of them may not work. So what's to be done?

- Should we verify each method separately? This approach is too long.

- Should we use different approaches in different tests? Then there is a possibility of missing some of the approaches.

One way to solve the problem is to choose the method for selecting a menu item in a random manner. For this purpose, we will write a separate function or method that will perform this operation. In this case, we do not have to verify explicitly all the methods, because one way or another each of them will be verified during one of the usual test runs. The more tests that are run and the more often the menu item operation is called, the more often each method will be verified.

At the same time, there is one important nuance. Since the method of action is chosen randomly, we must know exactly in the event of an error which method was chosen in the particular case leading to the error. For this purpose, you need to put in the log the information about which method was chosen, so that if you need to reproduce the problem, you can accurately reproduce the actions of the test.

1-10. Do Not Perform Blind Clicks Against Nonstandard Controls

Everyone sooner or later comes across a situation where some self-made control is not supported by the automation tool. After trying a few ways of testing such a control and not finding anything suitable, people stop at the simplest way of solving the problem: clicking on hardcoded coordinates. However, this is not always the best way.

Imagine a toolbox with several buttons. Let's assume that our tool does not recognize the buttons on the toolbox and does not see any properties or methods that would allow us to get their coordinates. If we hard-code the coordinates for a click inside the toolbar, then for a while our scripts will work. However, then something can happen (for instance, the order of the buttons or their size changes). In this case, the click will occur elsewhere.

One solution to the problem is to search for an image within another image that is provided by certain tools. We can save the image of the button (just the button rather than the entire toolbar), and then search for the button's image inside the image of the entire toolbar and click in the found coordinates. On the one hand, searching for an image is a time-consuming operation, but for small images the search will not last too long. On the other hand, even if a button changes its position or size, the search will still work correctly.

If your tool does not support searching for an image inside another one, then at least take such operations to a separate function. In your tests, there should not be such lines:

```
Window.Toolbar.Click(135, 15)
```

Instead, there should be a call to a function like the following:

```
toolbar_click_button_by_image(Window.Toolbar, "Button Caption")
```

It will be easier in this second case to understand the reason for any error that might occur during your test run. Your code will be clearer and more understandable as well.

1-11. Learn and Use Standard Libraries

Beginners in automation often make the mistake of creating something that has already been provided to them by the capabilities of the programming language or automation tool. Having been faced with some task, the tester starts writing his function or class to solve this task. Usually one's own version of a given functionality will be worse than the one already available and provided by the language or the tool.

Let's consider a simple example in Python. Let us suppose that we are working with Windows operating system, and we have a file path and file name in different variables; it is necessary to get the full path to this file. Here is how the newcomer solves this task:

```
file_path = 'C:\\Users\\tester\\'
file_name = 'picture.png'
full_name = file_path + file_name
print full_name
```

For a while, everything will be fine, but someday the file_path variable will lack a backslash character at the end. Then the tester will rewrite the code a little differently:

```
full_name = '{0}\\{1}'.format(file_path, file_name)
```

Now we always get the correct file name. Sometimes two slashes will appear between the folder and the file name, but the operating system correctly handles such situations. But do not lull yourself into believing we are done.

Over time, we have a new requirement: to compare the file name obtained by us with the same name in the tested application. As a result, we get an error in those names where we had a double slash between the folder and file name, and again solve our problem by modifying our function, this time with a call to a text replacement function:

```
full_name = '{0}\\{1}'.format(file_path, file_name)
full_name = full_name.replace('\\\\', '\\')
```

As you can see, with each new requirement our code becomes more and more complicated, and all these problems could be avoided initially, using the standard Python function:

```
full_name = os.path.join(file_path, file_name)
```

First, this approach of using what Python already provides is more simple, convenient, and understandable. Secondly, standard library functions are usually well tested and take into account a lot of small, corner cases that you are likely to miss when creating a new function with the same capabilities by yourself.

Therefore, always look for standard ways of solving problems first, and only if there is no such solution - create your own. Also, when faced with a new library for yourself, look at all of its capabilities. Glance over them, at least. Doing so will save you time in the future.

1-12. Avoid Copy and Paste

Copying and pasting of code in order to reuse it is a common mistake of beginners. Once you need to write a new code, you remember that you already wrote something similar in the past. You find your old code, change it a little, and create a new function.

Then again … again … and again…

Once you find an error in one of your copies, you correct it and understand that in all your copies there is the same problem. You spend the time to find all the places where the mistake was made.

Then it happens again … again … and again…

Once you are faced with a problem that needs to be corrected in the same way in several places, you must make sure that there is exactly one place left. Let it be a function that takes into account all the necessary options, or let it be a function with several parameters, but it must be only one function, with the code in one place.

Do not be too lazy to write code correctly. Be lazy now by copying and pasting, and in the future you will remember what I have said and regret doing so. You will spend an hour and regret that you once grudgingly spent an extra five minutes.

Have pity on yourself, do not copy and paste. If you use a popular programming language, it is likely that the language already has tools for detecting duplicate code. Use them!

1-13. Do Not Use try...catch with an Empty catch Block

Every programmer writes such a construction once:

```
try{/*some code*/}
catch()
{} /*ignore all exceptions and continue execution*/
```

Here, we execute certain code, completely ignoring all possible exceptions. This is acceptable for temporary code, when you are experimenting, but it is completely unacceptable in tests that run regularly.

It doesn't matter how simple the code is in the try block. Even if it's just one line, there might theoretically be an unexpected error, but you will never know about it. For this reason, the first correction will be that we will add an output message to the catch block:

```
catch(e)
{print(e.description)}
```

Now we will have the text of the exception in the log, and we'll be able to see it later when sorting out the logs and trying to understand what is going wrong.

A similar example is a large try block, and handling only one possible exception in the catch block. This will lead to the same result as in the first case, with the exception of the one processed case that is properly handled.

For such a situation, there is a right approach: intercept only those exceptions that you accurately need to handle, while not ignoring other possible errors. Catch the one error that you care about, and throw the other errors up the chain, like in this example:

```
catch(e)
{
  if(e.number == 123)
    {/*just ignore this*/}
  else
    {throw e}
}
```

If in the future you need to ignore (or handle in a different manner) other exceptions, you simply add a new else block for them.

Sometimes an empty catch block gets into a test accidentally. For instance, you add an empty catch block temporarily, plan to finish it a bit later. To avoid such accidents, just write the catch block right away, without leaving it for later.

1-14. Separate Code from Data

When we write tests, we need a place to store the expected values, which we compare to what the tested application actually produces. When dealing with a single piece of data (one number, text, etc.), we just use variables. For small datasets (for instance, items in the drop-down list), we can use arrays or lists. But what if there is a lot of data (for instance, several dozen values)?

It is inconvenient to store large amounts data along with the code, since the data simply obstructs the code. You can put the data in a separate code file, but in this case it is inconvenient to work with the data, because there is no vertical alignment in text files and, for instance, the lines will have different widths, which makes it difficult to understand the information.

You can solve all these problems by using the data-driven testing (DDT) approach. This is an approach in which data is stored in a separate file in the form of tables. It can be a database of any format, an Excel or comma-separated value (CSV) file.

Modern automation tools usually support working with one or more of these formats. For many programming languages, there are libraries that make it easier to work with such tables. If in your case there is nothing readily available, you can write simple functions to work with formats such as CSV.

Here are some tips for working with data using the DDT approach:

- open data files only in read mode from the tests. Since data files contain model data, changing it automatically during scripts run is potentially dangerous. If you need to change this data, you need to do this manually, knowing exactly what you are changing and why;

- store only one type of data in each column. In case of a database, you will not be able to do otherwise; however, in case of text files or Excel files, you will have to monitor it by yourself. Some Excel drivers can behave strangely if they encounter a value with a mismatched data type. In addition, your tests can also work with errors in case of inconsistency of data types;

- don't forget to close the connection to the data source file after you have finished reading the data from it. Leaving an open connection can prevent you from connecting to it from other tests;

- in case of using Excel files, make sure that the data is stored as in the database. For instance, if you leave an empty line in the middle of the table, the driver can consider it as the end of the file while reading data. Therefore, closely look after the data in the hidden lines, if there are such in your files.

It doesn't matter which type of data storage you choose. It is a good practice to keep your data separate from code.

1-15. Learn How to Debug

Debugging is a step-by-step execution of a program in order to detect an error in it. Learning to debug is easy. The basics of debugging can be studied in an hour, but the benefits of using it are huge.

KNOW YOUR TOOLS

Once I worked in a new team with a new tool for me and I could not step into a function in debug mode. After digging in a little bit, I found that the application editor simply "doesn't see" where this function is located, therefore it can't go into its source code. I asked the experienced (as I thought at that time) colleagues:

How can I go inside this function?

In no way. This tool does not know how to do this.

But how do you debug scripts?

Debug? Well ... We look carefully at the function and try to understand where the problem is.

It took me only half an hour to figure out how to "teach" our tool to go inside the function, then for another half hour I showed "experienced colleagues" how to use debugging tools. "Cool," they said.

Among novices, there are many such people who simply did not learn debugging, and therefore don't know that it is possible. That is why debugging is one of the mandatory things that I show during my trainings that I deliver to new people on my team.

Here are the basic concepts that you need to study and begin to use (these capabilities are available in any editor):

- Setting of breakpoints. A breakpoint is the place where execution of the program stops, waiting for action from you.

- Step-by-step debugging. This is what allows you to step forward in code, step backward, execute to a cursor, and watch each step of your program unfold.

- Viewing values of local and global variables. All debuggers provide mechanisms to examine the value of variables.

- Observation of variables and expressions. Debuggers often provide watch list functionality to let you know when the value of a variable or an expression changes.

Typically, there is a detailed description of all the debugging features in the help system of your development environment. Become familiar with that documentation so that you can explore features and take full advantage of what your debugger can offer you.

You can use any programming tutorial to understand the basics of debugging. However, there is one feature specific for automation only. If you are dealing with a variable that corresponds to a display object, the values of its properties will not always match the values during the test run. For instance, the Visible property can be set to False during debugging, because at that moment the editor itself is a top window. However, while the tests are running, the value of this property will be True, because the window with this element will be displayed on the screen, and the editor window will be hidden.

In addition, some actions in the step-by-step mode may not be performed. For instance, when you try to click on a specific object, your tool will not be able to move focus to the desired window. As a result, clicking will not happen.

In all other respects, debugging in test automation does not differ from debugging in programming.

1-16. Do Not Write Code for the Future

There are two ways in which to write tests:

- You write a test and, as you write it, you write the general functions and methods that will be used in this and future tests.

- You first write common functions and methods and then quickly develop a test that uses everything written before.

Each approach has its advantages and disadvantages. Each approach can be effectively used in different situations.

However, there is one approach that does not work: writing a lot of common code for many tests first and then starting using it. The key words here are "a lot": for example, if you are going to immediately write all the functions and methods for a dozen future tests.

Write for the present. Not for the future.

A TALE OF WASTE

In one project, we tried to write code with an eye toward all our possible future needs. We took a big piece of functionality that we were going to cover with tests and started planning the code that we might need. We thought through functions with parameters and return values; we looked at all the tests and their interaction with various application windows; we argued and reworked our plan, and then reviewed again.

We spent two days on planning and started to write the code. We spent two more weeks writing all the functions and classes, rechecked everything several times, and finally started to write tests.

First, we encountered minor changes that we had to make into the code already written, since we did not take into account something. Then we had to add a few new functions and completely redo some existing classes. And, finally, after writing all the tests, we removed all the code that was not immediately useful.

As a result of all that we wrote for two weeks, no more than one-third of the code (the most elementary of it) remained almost unchanged, another one-third we had to substantially redo, and we deleted the remainder. About a week's worth of work by several people was wasted.

1-17. Leave the Code Better Than It Was

The Boy Scouts have a rule: "Always leave the place cleaner than you found it." It is about the cleanliness of the campground: leaving, you need to leave it cleaner than it was before your arrival.

The same goes for someone else's code. If you stumble upon someone else's code that you can definitely improve without spending too much time – do it! Make the improvements. Such improvements can be simplification of a clearly tangled piece of code, or simply consist of syntax corrections (adding indents or extra lines to improve readability).

You only need to improve code if you are 100% sure that doing this will not affect the efficiency of the code or the results of its execution, and also if it does not take you more than a few minutes.

If this simple rule is followed by everyone, our tests will constantly improve and reading such code will be much more pleasant. Therefore, teach others the same by your example.

1-18. Choose a Proper Language for GUI Tests

Many automation tools offer a choice of several programming languages you can write tests in. And often people try to choose the same language for tests in which the application under test is written. This approach has a number of advantages:

- We don't produce programming languages without the need.

- Testers can always ask the programmers for advice.

- In case of necessity, programmers will be able to create and maintain tests.

- API testing is greatly simplified.

However, choosing the same language for tests as for the product being developed is not a strict rule. It is unlikely that programmers will ever look into the test code, so tests can be written in any language that is convenient for testers.

In addition, the tasks of testers are usually much simpler than the tasks of programmers. Writing a commercial application is much more difficult than writing tests for it. For this reason, allowing programmers to design a test engine can lead to complexities that can be avoided. Programmers might initially try to design such a system "with a margin for the future," trying to foresee what testers will never encounter. Therefore, you should be guided in choosing the programming language for GUI tests, first of all, by what your team will find more convenient and easier to work with, rather than by what your application under which the test is written in.

THE WRONG LANGUAGE

Nevertheless, for some types of automation, things can be quite different. In one of my projects it was decided to implement integration testing for a plug-in that works with mobile devices. All automation in the project was done using Python. The plug-in was written in C++. We wrote our tests in Python, only to later realize our work would have been easier in C++.

To develop the tests, programmers had to write wrappers that Python could work with (for this, the Boost.Python library was used). The testers, for their part, had to write wrappers that converted some types of Boost.Python variables into regular Python variables so that it was convenient to work with them.

In general, the preparatory work took three months, after which all the necessary tests were written within two weeks. Since neither developers nor testers had had experience doing such tasks, no one could estimate the time needed in advance.

When our little effort was over, everyone agreed that it would be simpler to write our tests in C ++, which would take the same two weeks. By writing in C++ we would not have needed to spend the additional three months in developing wrapper functions.

1-19. Remember to Declare and Initialize Variables

Many automation tools use scripting languages to create tests. In some of the tools, it is allowed to use variables without declaring them. In others you can initialize variables explicitly when they are declared.

For instance:

```
var myVariable;
```

or:

```
notDeclaredVar += 1;
```

Such simplifications can lead to unpleasant situations. If we do not initialize a variable when we declare it, we can't know exactly what value will be assigned to the variable. For this reason, any action with it can lead to an error that can't be reproduced later.

As for the possibility of using undeclared variables, doing so can lead to completely unexpected consequences.

LOST ELEMENTS

Once I spent two hours trying to figure out why, when bypassing elements in a tree control, some elements were simply skipped. And it was impossible to see any system in this, each time random elements were skipped. As a result, it turned out that I forgot to declare the loop variable inside the bypassing function, but there was a global variable with the same name. It was used in the loop, and its value depended on completely different factors that were not relevant to the current tree.

Therefore, if you do not want to encounter such strange mistakes, always follow two rules:

1. Always declare variables.

2. Always initialize them with initial values.

This applies even if declaration or initializing can be skipped in the language you use. Here is an example in JavaScript:

```
var myVariable = 0;
```

or:

```
declaredVar = 0;
declaredVar += 1;
```

In the first case we initialize a new declared variable, which is not mandatory in JavaScript. In the second example we assign a zero to a previously declared variable before starting using it in order to be sure the variable doesn't contain an unpredictable value.

CHAPTER 2

Testing

We use testing automation to improve the quality of the manual testing, speed up execution of functional tests, simplify regression testing, and avoid human mistakes during verifications. It makes automation a part of the whole quality assurance process, which means we should follow the same best practices in automation as we do in manual testing.

However, there are some rules we should take into account when automating existing test cases and user cases, or when we decide what should be automated and what should stay for manual execution. This chapter describes best practices related to the testing process and the relationship between manual and automated testing.

2-1. Do Not Duplicate Tested Application Functionality in the Scripts

An application under test performs calculations and outputs a result. How to check that the result is correct? The first option that comes to mind is to calculate the same in the test script and compare the result with what the application gives us! This approach is incorrect for several reasons:

- Calculations can be complex. The programmers have already spent time on them and now you will do the same.

- Formulas for calculations may change later. In this case you will see an error in the report, although the application works correctly. You will have to make corrections, again spending time for this.

- When working with floating-point numbers, the accuracy of calculations may differ in the language that you use for tests and in the language in which the application under test is written. As a result, you will have to artificially customize your calculations so that they coincide with the result of the application.

The correct approach in such situations is to calculate the correct result manually and save it in the script as expected. If one calculation is enough, then write its result directly in the script. If several calculations are needed, use arrays or the DDT-approach.

© Gennadiy Alpaev 2017
G. Alpaev, *Software Testing Automation Tips*, https://doi.org/10.1007/978-1-4842-3162-3_2

THE PERIL OF NO PARENS

As an example, consider the calculation of the expression 2 + 2 * 2 in Windows Calculator. In the standard mode, the result will be 8, and in scientific mode it will be 6. That's because scientific mode takes into account the precedence of operations.

Let's say you use a programming language that also follows precedence of operations. In your calculations, the result will always be 6. You will need to complicate the calculation of the expression by adding parentheses to it if you prefer the other possible result. In testing it is better to avoid repeating the math. Simply write your test code to expect whichever value you intend for the application under test to produce.

It is best if the source data and the correct results for them are given to you by competent people (for example, product specialists). Your responsibility is to code the test, but usually it should not be your responsibility to determine what the result should be.

Now if your test has failed, then either the application is not operating correctly, or something has changed in the requirements and you need to update the test data. Either way, you can be assured that the failure is not a problem of the test code!

If, for some reason, it is impossible to completely abandon such calculations, try to simplify and reduce them in tests as much as possible. Also, make sure to put some comments in the script or error message describing what was calculated and why it was done. It may help you or someone else who will be analyzing possible errors in the future.

2-2. Each Test Should Be Independent

Beginners often make an error while automating when one test uses data that was generated in another test. A vivid example of this is the CRUD functionality, when one test creates a record, another one edits it, and the third one deletes the record.

The only advantage of this approach is the time saving; however, several disadvantages appear at once:

- If the test that creates the record fails for some reason, then the rest will also fail.

- In the report you will see not one error, but several, although the functionality of editing and deleting can be correct.

- When the tests are started automatically, it's not always possible to ensure that they will run in a specific order.

If you want to save a little time and not have to create additional records using the application, you can do it otherwise. For instance, create them using an SQL query to the database, with the application API, or use the database in which the necessary entries are already created. In this case, to verify the independence of the tests from each other you can run the tests in a random order, if this can be implemented for your automation tool.

Another approach to solving the problem is to run first the test, which will create all the test data necessary in the future. However, if this test fails, then running all the others is meaningless, and as a result no test will be started at all.

If you still think that in your case the use of dependencies between tests is the most optimal approach, in each dependent test you should check the results of that test on which they depend, and do not run the dependent test if the previous one did not work correctly.

Another possible way to solve the problem is to combine several dependent tests into one.

2-3. What Should Not Be Automated?

In any project, there are tasks that need to be automated, but there are those that should be left for manual testing only. For each project, of course, such tasks will be different, but you can identify several common areas, which should not be automated.

- Do not automate something that is difficult to maintain. Even if you have already written a test, but you have to regularly fix and restart it, consider deleting it or simplifying it as much as possible.

- Do not automate someone else's application. For instance, if you need to work with Google mail, do not write complex code that will work with the interface of this mailer (of course, this does not apply to Google employees).

- Automation of the interface (its correctness and ease of use) is possible in principle, but too time consuming and usually incomplete.

- Interaction with any peripheral devices (printers, scanners, etc.) that require human participation is usually either complicated, or requires too much additional manual work.

- Verification of the correctness of various images, graphics, and video is also easier to perform manually.

- Obfuscated applications and individual components cannot be automated, since the names of their properties change at each compilation.

Nevertheless, sometimes it makes sense to combine automation with manual testing.

ADVANTAGE TO MANUAL

In one of my projects I had a fairly complex test, which was performed in automatic mode for about 20 minutes and manually for at least an hour. In addition, this test included various calculations and combinations of input parameters, which made the test very difficult for manual testing.

In the last step of this test, I had to change the time on the remote server and reboot it to perform the latest verifications. Technically, the task was solved, but approximately every third run failed for various reasons. Each time I had to look for a possible cause and fix it, since the problem was not reproduced manually.

After suffering for two months I solved the problem in a different manner. I decided to set a breakpoint before the last step, and then I commented the server restart code. Every morning I came to work, manually rebooted the server, and clicked the Continue Execution button only after I was sure that the server really rebooted, started, and the time on it was correct.

All those actions took me each time no more than 15 minutes (including setting the return date back on the server), and the test was no longer failing. Attempts to find and fix the cause of the fails took much more time than simply spending 15 minutes every day.

Do not consider the rules in the prior list to be an axiom. Just keep them in mind and try to find the most optimal solution to your problem. Sometimes the right solution is to break the rules, as I did when commenting out that restart code.

2-4. Ask the Developers for Help

The tests we write are simplified programming, which is necessary to simplify testing. Of course, you can make a complex framework, but in most cases this is not required. The same goes for other areas that programmers come across more often: regular expressions, working with databases, using internal application methods, and more. Therefore, usually programmers are more experienced in such things and can give useful advice in the rare cases when you need to develop more complex testing solutions.

If you are faced with a complex problem that you do not know how to approach, try to ask the advice of developers. Of course, it is not worth running for help with every little thing; it is often much more useful to understand by yourself, thereby increasing your experience.

ON ACCEPTING HELP

Sometimes it is useful to interact with developers even if you know the solution. Once I designed some tests and my solution seemed complicated. I talked with an architect for just five minutes and he suggested a simpler solution right away, as soon as I described the task and my solution to it. He was faced with designing much more than I did, he did not need to know the language I was writing on, or the features of test execution automation, to solve that particular problem.

However, always remember that the view of the programmer of the application is different from yours and not all pieces of advice are equally good. The programmer looks at the application from the inside and knows how it works. You look from the outside and know how it *should* work.

NOT ALL ADVICE IS GOOD ADVICE

In one project I consulted with developers how to get data easily from the table for verification. It was .NET application with GridView control. Developers advised me to work with the DataSet object in which the data for this table was stored, they even were ready to help me writing the code to extract the data, because they worked with it every day and it was not difficult for them.

However, from the testing point of view it was bad advice, because the DataSet object contains raw data and with its help I could verify just data. However, GridView element displays the data taking into account the user's local settings (for instance, depending on the operating system settings, different decimal symbols for digits or date format can be used), which, of course, must also be taken into account when testing.

This example shows the difference between developers' and testers' approaches to work with applications. That's why you better know what and how you should test, and programming issues should be discussed with the developers, thereby improving your skills.

2-5. Cloud Testing

In recent years, cloud services have become popular, providing the ability to run virtual machines in particular. Since these services are quite cheap, many people have a desire to run automatic tests in the clouds. Before making such a decision and starting the implementation, consider several important points:

- To test desktop applications, an open session is mandatory (it can be either a logged-in user or Remote Desktop session). If there is no such session, the operating system simply does not render applications' GUI, which means that the automation tools will not see a single window or control.

- In particular, the need for an open GUI means that you can't just configure a remote virtual machine and run tests on it, using, for instance, the command line. You will need to connect to the virtual machine using Remote Desktop and leave the connection window open for the duration of the tests. If during the operation the connection is interrupted for at least a second, the automation tool will not recognize the application elements, and this will lead to unforeseen errors.

- Any automation associated with physical devices is also inconvenient in the cloud, since you have no direct access to the physical devices your cloud provider is allocating to your account.

- Cloud services that provide access to mobile devices are more expensive than usual cloud virtual machines. Therefore, it is better to run automatic tests on local mobile devices, and cloud services should be used only for manual testing (for instance, to verify if the application works on a device that you don't have).

- Automation of web applications is best carried out in the clouds. It is only necessary not to return the virtual machine to the initial state, if at the end of the tests you need to verify something on this machine.

In general, working with virtual machines in the clouds is not as convenient and fast as with local computers and virtual machines. And given the comparative cheapness of computer hardware, for ordinary tasks you can use only local machines. Cloud services are needed when there are no other options (for instance, for emulating load testing).

2-6. Introduce Automation for Corner Cases

Let's assume that at a certain point in the test you need to enter a number from 1 to 10 into the field. Testing all 10 cases is quite expensive, so we select a random number and enter only it. If each time while running a test only this number is entered, we will have 9 potential errors that are never checked.

You can choose this number randomly from the range or test several values instead of 1, but in addition, you should always test the values 1 and 10. It is with these corner values there are often associated different errors, which programmers do not take into account during the development or writing of unit tests. Thus, in our automated test we will check at least 3 numbers: 1, 10, and any number in the range from 2 to 9 inclusive.

Of course, we also need to check that the application does not allow entering in this field negative, numeric, and other values that are not suitable for this field, but this already refers to negative testing, and we are talking about a positive one here.

2-7. The Difference Between Error and Warning

There are errors of two types: critical and non-critical. From an automation point of view, this means that if after an error occurs we can continue to run the test, then the error is not critical. It is these non-critical errors that are warnings.

Non-critical errors must be seen in the report in order not to forget about them; however they must be marked with a color different from the color of the critical errors. For instance, critical errors may be marked in red, and non-critical errors may be indicated by yellow.

Unfortunately, many tools generate reports in the JUnit format, which was originally intended for unit tests written by developers. These are small and very fast tests that usually check the correctness of individual functions and methods with different input parameters. Unlike GUI tests, a unit test can't have an intermediate state; it either passes or fails.

When the unit test engine is used for GUI testing, the test will be stopped at any error that appears. For instance, we verify the sorting in all columns of the table, for which we click on the column headers. If when clicking on one of the columns the data in this column will not be sorted – this is an error. However, this is not a reason to stop the test and not verify the remaining columns.

In order to solve this problem, in tools using JUnit reports, the following approach is used. Performing non-critical verification, in case of an error we simply add an error line to the error list (which is initially empty). At the end of the test, check this list. If it is still empty as it was in the beginning, then there are no errors in the test. If there are errors in the list, we mark the entire test as a failed one and put all the accumulated errors to the log.

If you have an opportunity to use reports that support warnings as one of the variants of the error – use them. It helps to easily distinguish critical errors from those which can be ignored at the moment.

2-8. Use the Appropriate Methodologies

There are a lot of specific methodologies that are used in testing automation: ODT, DDT, KDT, BDD, Page Objects, Model-Based Testing, etc. However, it is not enough to just know them; you need to use them appropriately.

Following are two vivid examples of misuse of methodologies on different projects.

Example 1

In a small project, the team decided to implement automation and employed an experienced automation engineer who previously worked for a large company where the automation was handled by a large department. The experienced automation engineer implements in the new project the same approaches that were used in his previous company; in particular, he uses Keyword-Driven Testing. Since the selected tool does not support this approach, the automation engineer writes it "from scratch" and fully supports it, and also automates existing manual tests.

What is wrong with this approach? It is wrong by the fact that the Keyword-Driven methodology is needed in those projects where the script code is written by one people, and the tests are written by others. If in the project only one person is fully engaged in the automation, then the support for the KDT approach will take 2/3 of the time, and only 1/3 of the time will be spent on creating the test.

In addition, if in the future this person leaves the project, and a less experienced automation engineer comes in his place, it will be very difficult for him to support this approach and eventually he will cease to use it.

Example 2

In the second example, we also deal with a small team with an equal number of programmers and testers. The customer really likes the possibility of test automation and he does everything possible to promote this idea. However, the customer's knowledge is limited to promotional materials, which are provided by companies that develop automation tools. These materials always say that it is enough to record the actions with the help of the tool, after which the tests will work fine. As a result of such misinformation, the customer requires testers to perform large amounts of work every week. To cope with the load, testers mainly use recording, only occasionally making changes to the recorded tests.

The Downside and How to Avoid It

The disadvantage of the approach taken in the examples is obvious: tests too often have to be changed, and they end up spending a lot of time on it. Sometimes it is easier to just rewrite them again, if the existing functionality has been greatly changed. The efficiency of such automation is very close to zero. Therefore, every time starting a new project or taking on a new task, try to think about what you will need, and what you can refuse.

2-9. Verification of Individual Bugs

In most cases, tests are written to verify some functionality in general and do not verify special cases, for instance, a bug with specific data. However, sometimes it happens that once corrected bug appears again after some time; the reasons for its appearance can be completely different, but the result looks the same. In such cases, it makes sense to write a separate test to verify this particular bug, or a separate test to verify several bugs.

The peculiarity of such bugs is that they do not fit into manual test scripts, and therefore can only be found by chance. Often such errors occur in actively developing projects, where several programmers can work on modifying the same functionality, therefore affecting each other's changes. If you write such a test, then in the report it is necessary to indicate the number of the existing bug in the bug tracker so that you can see the history of its findings and fixes. You can act the same way when you write an automated test and find an error in the application under test. You register a bug, and specify its number in the comment to the verification in the new test. Once such a bug is fixed, the error simply disappears from the report.

2-10. Make a Pilot Project Before Writing Real Tests

A pilot project is a project that lasts one-two months and is only needed for informational purposes. Pilot projects are used in several cases:

- if you are using a new automation tool for the first time;

- if you automate a new type of project (for instance, you had always worked with web applications, and now move on to testing the desktop or mobile applications);

- when implementing automation in a project where it did not exist before, and it is necessary to quickly show a certain result to the management or the customer.

The purpose of the pilot project is to try the tool, to understand its capabilities, and to study the main advantages and disadvantages. Therefore, expect that at the end of the pilot project you will delete it entirely (or almost entirely), since usually this project does not use the best approaches.

For a pilot project, you usually select a few simple tests and one-two tests of average difficulty. If your application uses complex controls (editable grids, specific controls, etc.), then at least one test should work with such an element. If this is not done right away, then it can later turn out that this tool can't work with such objects at all, which can significantly complicate the automation process.

Also, pilot projects are useful for training new team members, if they did not work in the field of test automation before. It will help the beginners to try to create their first projects from scratch and learn the basics before starting working with real projects together with other team members.

CHAPTER 3

Environment

There are two main types of environments in software testing automation. The first of them is the one we use to create and debug tests, and another one is used for running tests against tested applications. This chapter contains tips that will help you simplify your everyday job and set up proper environment infrastructure both for the local working place and server.

3-1. Choose a Proper Set of Tools for Your Needs

In my practice, I met two different types of people. Some tried to solve all their problems with the help of one tool, while others, for each new task, took something new. All of them had their own arguments. The first believed that since they had experience working with one particular tool, it is with its help that they would solve the problem most quickly. Others held the view that for each task there was the most suitable tool, and it was necessary to use it, even if no one in the team had experience with this tool.

As is usually the case, the truth is somewhere in the middle. Each of these types of people faced various difficulties. The decisions of the first were sometimes too bulky and complex, and it was very difficult for anyone, other than the author, to support them. The problem of the others was that it was very difficult to set up the working environment, and it required a lot of time and consultations with the author.

The most obvious is the following solution: find yourself a tool that will cover most of your needs and find one to two additional tools for everything else. Do not arrange a "zoo" of languages, tools, and libraries in your project, but do not try to solve everything with a single tool.

© Gennadiy Alpaev 2017
G. Alpaev, *Software Testing Automation Tips*, https://doi.org/10.1007/978-1-4842-3162-3_3

SIMPLIFYING TOOL SELECTION

I got to work in a project where the tool dilemma was solved quite simply. The only condition for automation and other auxiliary tasks was the use of the Python language. As a result, we had an application written in C++, and everything else was solved with the help of Python.

The programmers used Python for builds and assistant needs. We also had several libraries for testing Win32 applications: there was a separate tool for testing Qt-application, there were self-written API testing frameworks, but they all used Python.

As a result, the study and selection of new tools were simplified when they were needed, and the requirements for candidates were reduced when we were looking for new people in the project.

3-2. Do Not Automatically Register Bugs from Scripts

If the automation tool has integration with a bug tracker, one day you might have a wonderful idea: to automatically create a bug if there was an error in the script. Usually this makes no sense, since most errors in automated scripts are due to imperfections of the scripts themselves, or due to random events in the system on which tests are run. Errors also can be from use of the automation tool, due to the fault of the test author, from incorrect configuration, and only occasionally due to a real problem in the application. This is one of the reasons why automatic bug creation is a bad practice in test execution automation.

The second reason to avoid automatically registering bugs is that it is very difficult to write correct steps to reproduce a problem. You can't just write "run a test like this and at the end look at the error log." Programmers need clear instructions to reproduce the error that they can do on their computer in debug mode.

There is another solution. You can create tasks in the bug tracker automatically if an error occurs, but the person responsible for the error investigation should be the author of the test. If, for instance, tests are run at night, then in the morning the tester will first look if he has received new bugs during the night that are worth investigating first.

However, in this case, there are hidden pitfalls as well. If we have a problem with the test environment and no tests have passed, then for each of them a separate bug will be created. As a result, in the morning each tester will have a huge number of new tasks created overnight. If this happens on frequent occasions, after a while, people will just start to ignore such notifications. In this case, it makes sense to find the "golden mean": for instance, generate a template for a new bug, which will then be viewed manually, edited if necessary, and created in a bug tracker.

3-3. Do Not Chase After a "Green Build" in the Prejudice of Quality

Avoid the need to comment out a problem section of test code. Also avoid temporarily changing an expected result just so that a test runs to completion without appearing to fail. Here's an example of the sort of conversation that can lead to these two mistakes:

'Why do we have red build for three days?'

'Tests fail on a known issue.'

'Then fix it!'

'Not this week, maybe the next one, the problem is not critical there.'

'If the problem is not critical, why is the build red? Make sure it's green!'

The worst thing that a tester can do in this situation is to comment out a problem verification or worse: to temporarily make its current result an expected one. Often such changes from temporary become permanent, and in a year it is already impossible to understand why a deliberately wrong result is considered correct, or why the necessary verification is commented out.

Certainly, if a build is red for a long time - this is a problem, because people get used to this and feel normal. However, solutions to this problem need to be controlled. For instance, you can add a failing test to be quarantined. Then the results of the build will clearly show that there are quarantined tests. Another option is to disable a failing test in a way that is noticeable in the results. You can specify the number of the bug in the test comment due to which the test is disabled. The bug number can also be used to notify any change of the status of the bug to the person who disabled the test.

If you take the approach of disabling tests, then it makes sense to determine some threshold percentage that you choose not to exceed. For instance, you might consider that having 95% of the tests are working tests as the norm. Then if you noticed that more than 5% of your tests are disabled, you can consider that high number of disabled tests to be a problem.

3-4. Learn the Tool You Work With

Modern development environments provide great capabilities; however, many autotesters do not even use the main ones. It may be just simple actions we use several times every day or hour. *I have repeatedly seen how people use the mouse to select the menu item Edit | Comment Block or commented several lines one by one, instead of pressing a simple key combination and comment out the entire selected block.* In other cases, the functionality may be present in the editor, but its use may not be entirely obvious. You may use your IDE for years, having no idea that it contains something you needed from the very beginning.

THE VALUE OF SURPRISE FEATURES

In one of the tools that I used for several years, I was very short of conditional breakpoints. After two years of work, I accidentally clicked the right mouse button on the breakpoint icon and saw the menu item Condition. I was looking for something like this in the main application menu. Moreover, by studying the possibilities of conditional breakpoints, I came across another ability of this tool, which I had no idea about before.

In addition to simple things (such as working with code), editors can provide more advanced features: automatic code refactoring, connection of additional plug-ins, setting up different types of editor for normal mode and debugging mode, and much more.

Therefore, first of all, learn your tool – try everything you can find in it. And second, if you are missing something, try to find a solution: first in the built-in help system, then on the Internet. It is quite possible that what you need is simply called differently, and you just do not know about it.

3-5. Make Use of Version Control Systems

If you have not used a version control system before, you must begin right now. If you think that such a trifle as automatic tests shouldn't be stored in version control system, you are mistaken.

You can't just store your tests on your hard drive, as the tests become more and more time consuming, and one day you can lose them all if the hard disk goes out of order. Simply creating a copy of tests on another computer is a primitive analog of a version control system, so spend one day studying a real version control system and then begin using it, gradually improving your knowledge.

Usually, developers already use some kind of control system, so just start using that same system as well. You can store your tests in the same place where programmers store their source code, or use a separate project for tests. In various projects, this or that approach will be more convenient. Using the same system as your developers means that you can learn from them, and possibly vice versa.

However, keep a close eye on what exactly you put into your version control system. Some programming languages (even scripting languages) can generate binary files to speed up the work. These files are copies of scripts, but they do not need to be saved, since they are generated automatically and for the version control system are just rubbish.

Also, some tools can create separate files in which user settings are stored. Such files should not also be stored in the version control system, since everyone likes to customize the development environment for themselves and storing these settings in the version control system can interfere with other project participants.

3-6. Avoid Custom Forms

In some automation tools there is such a feature as custom forms. Especially often they are found in commercial instruments.

A custom form is a normal window that appears at a certain point during the test run and is intended for entering any information by user. In some projects, these forms are used to enter test parameters that will be used (for instance, server address, user name, etc.).

In most cases, the use of such forms is not recommended as well as any user interaction with automatic scripts. Tests should be run regardless of the person's presence, so that it can be done automatically, for instance, during nonworking hours (at night or on weekends). To stop the test at the right time, you need to use debug mode and breakpoints.

As for the test startup parameters, they can be stored in configuration files (for instance, ini, xml, and others). Changing these parameters in a file is as easy as entering them into a custom form. If different parameters are used on different computers (for instance, the user name on the current machine), you can use several parameter files, each of which corresponds to the name of the current computer.

3-7. Simplify Everything You Can

You work with a lot of things: tests, code, test environment, virtual machines, SQL queries, test data, reports, and more. It is very important that everything that you work with is simple. This is important both for yourself and for those who will work with it after you. So if something you are working with seems to be complicated, simplify it!

If you have a difficult test and you have to think through for a long time what exactly it does - break it down into several simple tests. If you have complex code and you have to debug it for a long time, simplify this code (for instance, break it into several separate elementary functions). And so on.

Anything that seems difficult or requires a lot of additional actions needs to be simplified. If you solve a problem and find a solution - do not rush to implement it, try to find an easier solution. Often the first way to solve the problem is not the simplest. By thinking for another half an hour, you can save yourself a half-day job.

One of the best ways to find a simpler solution to the problem is to consult with someone who works with you. An outside point of view can give impetus to thinking in a different direction.

For instance, you are looking for a way to automatically close some unnecessary applications on your computer before you start the nightly test run. Instead of writing complex code to find and close all possible applications, you can simply force the computer to restart before running the tests, and then at the time of the test startup, you will not have anything open except for your own tool that runs the tests.

Another example of simplifying the task is described in Chapter 2, in the section "What Should Not Be Automated?" Instead of spending several hours every week on fixing the tests, we simply perform part of the task manually, spending a few minutes.

These examples show that the best solution is not always to improve the existing approach. The best solution can be found if you transfer the problem to a different plane.

3-8. Automate Any Routine

I often meet strange people who work in automation, but can perform other daily tasks in the most inconvenient way. For instance, to start the program they open the Explorer, find the necessary folder in it, and run the program. They do this several times a day, rather than just make a shortcut on the taskbar or start by pressing a certain keyboard combination.

In another case, to start a program with many parameters from the command line, the person opens the console, goes to the desired folder, and manually writes the program name and all its parameters, although the same can be done 10 times faster if you write a batch file.

There are many such examples: people enter huge data sets manually, instead of writing a simple script and executing it; use the mouse where it would be 10 times faster to use the keyboard combination; use simple programs such as Notepad instead of more advanced editors, etc.

Your automation tool is not the only means by which you can automatize routine tasks. Use everything available! Once you have a regular routine task, think about how it can be speeded up or automatized. Using such approaches will not only improve your work speed, but will also improve your knowledge of the operating system you work in.

CHAPTER 4

■ ■ ■

Running, Logging, Verifying

When running your tests against tested application, it is very important to have a detailed report with comprehensive messages about any issues tests faced during the run. It is also important to decide how to organize your tests' run and how often tests should be run. This chapter describes some of the best practices in software testing automation related to running tests and creating logs for further investigation.

4-1. Run Scripts as Often as Possible

Generally, it is useful to run tests when a new build appears. But what's the use of the tests if they are unstable and fail with errors even if the application runs correctly?

When a test is just created, there may be a lot of unforeseen details in it. For instance, will the test work normally on a slower computer, in a virtual machine, with other settings, or with a slower network connection? And vice versa? How will the test work in the better test environment? What happens if the amount of data on the server is different each time and the speed of the application changes every time?

To stabilize your tests, run them as often as possible. The more often they run, the more likely you are to spot problems and immediately fix them.

There is no need to run tests each time on different builds. You can use the same build for multiple runs. This is especially true at the stage of introducing automation, when there are not many tests and it doesn't take much time to complete them all. It will become more difficult to run all tests when you have more and more tests in suite, but if you run scripts often and fix different tests-related issues, then in time your tests will be much more stable, and there will be no need for such regular runs on the same build.

Running scripts often is especially helpful for tests that work for a long while and depend on many factors, or in which a large number of verifications are performed. Such tests should be debugged the most thoroughly, as in the future you may want to run them not very often (for instance, once a week, not for each build), so they must be very reliable.

© Gennadiy Alpaev 2017

G. Alpaev, *Software Testing Automation Tips*, https://doi.org/10.1007/978-1-4842-3162-3_4

4-2. Perform an Automatic Restart of Failed Tests

Sometimes tests fail when running them automatically, but pass when running each of the failed tests separately. One of the possible reasons is the error that appears when the application is being used for a long time, or the problem with specific scenarios. Such cases need to be investigated to find their causes and reproducible scenarios and then to be fixed.

But sometimes such problems arise because of the specific test environment or the interaction of the automation tool with the application under test. In such cases, tests can hang for no apparent reason or simply report strange-at-first-glance errors that cannot be reproduced. If this is the case, it's necessary to do an automatic restart of tests that fail for unknown reasons. Such a process should look like this:

1. During the test run, the name of each failed test is added to the list.

2. After all the tests have worked, we must restart our automation tool.

3. We individually run each of the fallen tests, recording the results separately from the first results.

4. Then we manually review the results.

If one of the tests still regularly fails, it makes sense to look more closely at what the problem may be. If you cannot see the obvious problem, but the tests were successful the second time, you can consider them successful.

Be careful, however! There is always a possibility that the test fails for the first time due to errors in the test itself or the tested application, and restart of the test is nothing more than hiding the problem. In such cases, however, it makes sense to understand the causes of errors and eliminate them. To identify such tests, you should keep statistics on all startups and from time to time view it for the presence of "suspicious" tests.

4-3. A Disabled Test Should Be Provided with a Comment

Sometimes you have to temporarily disable an existing test. For instance, the need to disable can occur if the test produces an error that affects other tests, or the corresponding functionality is temporary disabled in the application under test.

When disabling a test, you should necessarily write a comment to the disabled test, so that any person, stumbling upon it, immediately knows the reason for the disabling. The comment should indicate the author of the disabling, the date, and the reason (preferably with the defect number, if such was entered in the tracking system).

Comments on disabled tests will help the author of the disabling (if, after a long time, you have to remember the reasons for the disabling) as well as other testers (for instance, if the author leaves the company and the connection with him is lost).

You can go further and implement an automatic verification of whether the corresponding defect is relevant at the time of the test run. If the defect is already closed, you can either automatically run the test, or generate an error stating that the test should be enabled.

It is also useful to view the disabled tests from time to time and update them, if necessary. For instance, after some time the functionality that was tested by the disabled test can be completely removed from the application. In this case, it makes no sense to store the corresponding test.

4-4. Errors in Logs Should Be Informative

Imagine that you come to work, open the nightly test reports, and you see an error message like the following:

```
ERROR: incorrect value
```

What does the text of the error tell you? Nothing!

There are a few components missing: the expected value, the actual value, the place where the error occurred, and the actions that led to this result.

For instance, we test a simple Calculator application such as you might find in Windows or in OS X by entering a lot of different mathematical expressions and verifying the results. An informative error message would look like this:

```
ERROR verifying result for expression "2+2*2". Expected: "6", actual: "8"
```

Pay attention to the quotation marks that enclose the values. They are not mandatory, but it is desirable to use them in case there are spaces or other nonprinting characters at the beginning or end of the line. When each of the values is quoted, similar problems are easier to discover.

If possible, you can also arrange the expected and actual values on different lines, one under the other. In this case, it's also easier to see the differences, especially in the case of long strings.

4-5. Make a Screenshot in Case of Error

No matter how detailed your logs are, nothing will replace a screenshot taken at the time an error occurred. This is especially true in GUI applications where the following occur:

- It is always easier to understand the error visually.

- It happens that the application under test is affected by something that could not be foreseen (for instance, there appeared a system message that caught the focus).

Some automation tools go further, suggesting you to create a screenshot each time the automation tool interacts with the tested application. Doing so is not recommended, because such a large number of pictures increases the size of the log, and the need for these screenshots is extremely rare.

If your tool does not have the option of automatic screenshot in case of an error – extend its capabilities by yourself so that it happens automatically. At the same time, pay attention to some features of different types of applications:

- Desktop applications rarely contain scrolling pages. All controls are usually either placed in one window, or several transitions between different windows are used with the help of a Next button.

- With web applications, a long page you need to scroll through to see all the content is quite common. You might want any screenshots to capture the entire scrolling region.

Often, tools allow you to take either a screenshot of the screen or a page, and for these actions you may need to call different functions. Therefore, when working with a web application and saving a screenshot, always think of what kind of information you need.

If you need the content of the entire page, then save the page exactly. If you need a screenshot (for instance, to see not only the browser window, but also other applications), then use the method of saving the entire screen, while remembering that some of the page content may not fit into the image.

4-6. Check the Accuracy of Tests Before Adding Them to the Regular Run

So, you wrote a test and it runs successfully. Let it be a simple calculator test that tests the expression "2 + 2". It will look like this:

```
function test_calculator()
{
  calculate(2+2);
  verify_result(4);
}
```

How can you guarantee that the test will output an error if suddenly the result is five? The solution is simple: change the expected value from 4 to any other value and run the test again. Do this for each verification. Do you like the result? Then feel free to put the test in the version control system and add it to regular runs to the rest of the tests, but don't forget to return the correct expected values before that!

There are more complex cases. For example, when a window is filled with data, close the window manually. How will the test behave? How will your automation tool behave as a whole?

You need to make sure that your tests behave correctly in difficult conditions, and your automation tool doesn't freeze or crash. When the tests and the tool behave predictably, it is always easier to quickly understand the causes of failed tests.

4-7. Avoid Comparing Images

Very often novice automation engineers make the mistake of comparing images rather than results. For example, they cannot check the individual properties of a control, so they verify a screenshot of the element, or even of the entire window, against a known good image of the element or window.

This approach of comparing screen shots is bad for several reasons:

- The slightest change in the appearance or size of an element leads to an error.

- Comparing images is much slower than comparing the properties of the same element.

- Updating the expected results for such verification points is usually more time consuming than updating the properties.

Usually verification of screenshots of the elements results from a lack of knowledge of the automation tool (provided, of course, the tool supports the type of your application under test and this particular control). It is better to spend a few days figuring out how to work with your application than to spend several hours a week in the future on supporting what you can avoid in general.

THE TIME SINK OF IMAGE VERIFICATION

The most terrible project that I saw used image verification in 50% of cases, because there was no other way to work with the application. The tests ran almost all night, although they did not do much work. Every week about a day of work was spent on investigating and updating the expected values, although there were no changes in the application!

Sorting out tools a little bit and reading the help system together with the programmers, we found out that only some small changes were needed to the tested application to avoid the need to compare screenshots. After making those changes, it was possible to reduce the working time of all tests by half, significantly facilitating their further support.

Nevertheless, although verification of screenshots is considered a bad style in automation, there are several cases when the approach can be used:

- Some tools work only with screen shots; this makes them universal for any application; however they are relatively slow and their tests are less stable.

- If you are testing an application that works with graphics, then the comparison of screenshots is usually the only possible approach for performing verifications.

- If you still can't work with the control, it is better to use screenshots than blindly click on the coordinates of the window.

In these cases, it usually makes sense to set up the advanced settings if they are provided in your automation tool. Settings to look for include the following:

- Inaccuracy confidential interval (may be called threshold or tolerance) – allows you to ignore a certain number of differences, specified in pixels or percentages.

- Transparency – allows you to specify an area inside the screenshot that must be ignored during the verification (for instance, there may be a Date field, which changes every day).

- Partial comparison – compare not a screenshot of the entire control, but only the significant part of it (for instance, for a button it is enough to verify the area where the text is located).

The set of available options depends on the tool you use. Some tools provide a wide set of options for image comparison, while others don't have any options at all. If you are unlucky enough to use a tool without necessary options, you can write your own functions to perform comparison of the images, though it may be a tricky task to implement.

CHAPTER 5

Reviewing

The review process is a good way to keep your code clear and understandable. It is important both to review others' code and having your own code reviewed, not depending on how many years you have been working in the project or how much experience you have gotten. This chapter describes several cases when it is important to review or optimize your tests, or vice versa – when it is better to do nothing instead.

5-1. Write Tests That Even Non-Automation Engineers Can Understand

Tests should be well written in order to be easy to maintain and modify, as well as to make it easy for you to find the reasons behind any failures during execution. How then, does one determine if a test is well written or not?

One approach is for the automation engineer writing a test is to show it to a tester who is not familiar with programming. If the tester understands what the test does, then the test is considered to be good.

Achieving clarity is very simple. Simply take care to write each test using function names that speak for themselves. For example:

```
function test_login()
{
  open_page("http:\\mywebsite.org");
  login_as(login="test user", password="test password");
  verify_page_opened("Web Site Start Page");
}
```

This code will be understandable even for those who are not familiar with programming. No matter how complicated the internal implementation of the invoked functions is, everything is clear at the top level.

© Gennadiy Alpaev 2017

G. Alpaev, *Software Testing Automation Tips*, https://doi.org/10.1007/978-1-4842-3162-3_5

For comparison, record such actions using any automation tool and look at the result. You will get something like the following:

```
driver = self.driver
driver.get(self.base_url + "/admin/")
driver.find_element_by_id("fLogin").clear()
driver.find_element_by_id("fLogin").send_keys("my-email@example.com")
driver.find_element_by_name("pass").clear()
driver.find_element_by_name("pass").send_keys("MY PASSWORD")
driver.find_element_by_css_selector("button.saveButton.okButton").click()
```

You should admit that this code is not only longer, but also less understandable in comparison with the first version. Automated recording tools will tend to generate code that is unclear and difficult to understand, whereas writing tests with intention allows you to invoke functions having clear names and purposes.

5-2. Avoid Unneeded Optimization

I have seen many times that testers are doing an unnecessary thing: they optimize the speed of a particular function, because it seems to them that it does not work fast enough. Before starting to perform any optimization, you need to make sure it provides benefits that are worth spending time on to optimize your code.

HOW IT LOOKS

Usually the unneeded optimization effort looks something like this:

1. An application starts for 3 seconds, then for 5 seconds the test script fills in fields for searching, there is another 5 seconds for the search process, after which for 1 second the script reads the found data and verifies it.

2. The tester begins to optimize the reading and verification functions (since he can't optimize the application under test).

3. The tester spends a day of work on optimization and achieves run times of half a second each for the reading and the verification.

Indeed, the test engineer has doubled the productivity of his code, but as a result he got a win of about 5% in the overall scheme. The gain is not obtained for all tests, but only for those that use the optimized functions. It's hardly worth it to spend a day on such optimization, especially if the tests are run at night and it does not matter if they work at night for 5 hours or for 5 hours and 1 minute.

According to the Theory of Constraints, optimization should always begin with the weakest section. In the test automation, this section is usually the application under test. Not always, but often. Optimization of test scripts is often free from providing any benefit.

Of course, you do not need to always use the slowest algorithm if you know another that happens to be faster. And I am not saying that you don't ever need to optimize. There is a time for optimization.

What I suggest is that you optimize tests in two cases:

- If a test runs unreasonably long, and the application under test is idle during the test execution.

- If you see an obvious problem in the code, the correction of which doesn't take much time.

You should always look at the performance of the scripts from the point of view of the whole system (scripts, the application under test, and the environment on which the testing is performed). For this purpose, at the very beginning of the project, it is better to determine the quality criteria that automatic tests should meet (speed of all tests, the frequency of running certain tests, etc.) and follow those criteria.

5-3. Review Someone Else's Code Regularly

Viewing a new code written by another person is one of the best ways to keep your project in order. As soon as a test and the general functionality necessary for it are written, the code should be looked at by a second person. It is possible during such reviews to find potential errors, or simply to fix incomprehensible or difficult places in the code.

Code written by junior testers must especially be checked. The code of more experienced employees also needs to be reviewed, however, since no one is fail-safe. Sometimes it happens that the author of code for a test has made some assumptions that are incorrect. Other times a developer might mock up some functionality intending to fix it later, but forgets to do it. Reviews can help catch such problems.

There is no need during the review stage to verify whether a test works, since such verification should be made by the author of the test. You only need to view the code itself and pay attention to complex or incomprehensible blocks. To do this, you can make a small list of rules, helping you focus on what to look for when reviewing.

Viewing someone else's code also has the reverse side: it is quite possible that by reading it you will find something new, a simpler algorithm or approach that you did not know about or just did not use for a while.

Another good example is pair programming, in which one person writes the code, and another one sits nearby and gives advice. Although at first glance it may seem that this approach leads to a loss of time for one of the participants, the overall quality of such code is higher than when one person writes it.

5-4. Participate in Forums and Discussions

If you are a beginner in automation and come to work in an automation team, you will learn a lot from your colleagues. However, it may happen that you are the only automation engineer in the company, or in your department, and there is no one around who to provide advice in a difficult moment. The solution? Help others! There is no better way to speed up your learning.

In these cases, specialized forums dedicated to the automation tool that you use will help you. Many people are limited to just asking questions on such portals; however, answers to questions are the minimum such forums can give you. Of course, you will probably start with a question, and, most likely, you will immediately get an answer, since the questions of newcomers can usually be resolved fairly quickly.

Subscribe to new messages from your forum of choice, and carefully read both questions and the answers to them. In time, you will see that the answers to some questions are clear to you, and that some of the questions you can answer yourself. Once you feel that you know the right answer, feel free to write the answer! The worst thing that can happen is you will be mistaken, you will be corrected by more experienced participants, and you will become even more experienced.

After a while you will be able to answer many questions. If you are not sure of the correctness of a particular answer that you plan to provide, then try it yourself to be sure. Even if you are not sure of the correctness of your own solution, it still makes sense to try to solve a problem by yourself before checking others' answers.

Such a study on other people's examples will give you the opportunity to work with those tool options that you might never have encountered at work. For instance, if you are testing only desktop applications, you will never encounter web applications, and your knowledge of the tool will be one-way. If in the future you will go to interview in another company, where they test the web applications, you will be surprised how weak your knowledge is.

On the contrary, if you regularly try to solve other people's tasks, you will accumulate diverse experience. And once, when faced with a task for the first time, you will know exactly how to solve it, although you have never done anything like this before.

MY EXPERIENCE FROM HELPING

I know that this method of forum participation and helping others works, because I learned one of the tools I use in my work by following precisely the advice given in this tip, being the only automation engineer in the company at the time. Later I wrote two textbooks on that tool, and for several years conducted training on its use.

5-5. Perform Refactoring

Refactoring is the simplification of existing code, in which the functionality of the application does not change (and in the case of test automation – the functionality of the tests or common code). Despite the fact that the code in test automation is usually much simpler than in real applications, sometimes you still need to do refactoring.

- You may find that the code you are supporting is too complex. This is a good candidate for refactoring.

- There may be a request for writing new tests, for which there are already almost suitable common functions and classes. In this case, it is better to make changes to the existing code than to write a new one (probably repeating the same errors as the author of the original code).

- Refactoring may be needed to improve the code that was written in a hurry. Such tests can't be left in the form they were written; it is necessary to immediately plan their modification and bring them to an acceptable form.

Since refactoring should not change the functionality of the tests, it is required to run all the tests that use the modified code immediately after refactoring is done. It is even better to simulate errors in tests to make sure that tests continue to perform those verifications that were performed before refactoring.

Programmers often use unit tests to make sure that changes in code do not affect the results of their work. In test automation, this is not always convenient, because functions and classes can work with screen elements, that is, to verify this code, you will need to run the application under test. However, if you have libraries that don't depend on GUI elements, you can also use unit tests in your project.

If you are not familiar with refactoring, take any book on this topic and read at least about the basic methods. Most probably you will be using just five to six refactoring methods in your everyday work, so you should master these methods and have a quick look at other ways of refactoring just in case.

5-6. Remove Tests That Provide Minimal Benefit

Imagine that your application under test is actively developing, and you are constantly writing new tests. Over time, the support for existing tests will take more and more time, with less time to write new ones. Then you will have a choice: either significantly reduce the writing of new tests, or delete some of the old ones, the benefits of which are minimal.

The first approach is not suitable. You cannot reduce writing new tests, because you need to try to cover with automated tests as much functionality as possible. Thus, the approach that is left is to remove older tests that are providing minimal benefits.

How do you determine whether a test is useful or not? To do this, it is necessary to keep statistics on each available test as early as possible. Track statistics such as the following:

- How many times each test was started;

- How many real problems were found by a given test;

- How often the test has to be fixed.

In time, you will see that not all tests are equally useful. You will find that some tests are helping you to find more bugs, whereas other tests seem to do little more than use up your valuable time in keeping them maintained.

For instance, some problems are easily detected manually, and therefore they are registered before the corresponding tests are started. It can also happen that several tests verify the same functionality, making one or more of those tests redundant.

In such cases, you can't just throw off the "most useless" tests. It is necessary to review each such test manually in order to understand the probable cause of its "uselessness". Only then can you make a decision about its removal, or transfer to manual testing. Try to involve all automation participants in your project in the process, since everyone should feel responsible for the overall work.

It may be difficult for you to delete the results of your own work, but it is better to have 10 tests that can be supported than 50 tests that are generating so many results that you do not have time to figure out the reasons of their fails and correct the situation.

Index

A

Accuracy, tests, 40
Automatic restart, failed tests, 38

B

Behavior-driven development (BDD), 6

C

Cloud testing
    automatic, 26
    implementation, 26
    virtual machines, 26
Comma-separated value (CSV) file, 14
Custom forms, 35

D

Data-driven testing (DDT) approach, 14
Debugging, script, 15–16
Disabled tests, 38–39

E, F, G, H, I, J

Environment
    advanced features, 34
    automation, 36
    avoid custom forms, 35
    capabilities, 33
    disabling tests, 33
    infrastructure, 31
    problem verification/worse, 33
    register bugs, scripts, 32
    simplify, 35
    sort of conversation, 33

tools, 31, 32
version control system, 34
Errors
    logs, 39
    screenshot, 39

K, L, M, N, O, P, Q

Keyword-driven testing (KDT), 6, 28

R

Refactoring performance, 47
Review process
    avoid unneeded optimization, 44–45
    participation, forums and
        discussions, 46
    refactoring, 47
    removal, tests, 47–48
    someone else's code, 45
    written tests, 43
Running scripts, 37
Running test
    accuracy, 40
    automatic restart, failed tests, 38

S

Scripting
    automation, 5–6
    BDD/KDT, 6
    bulky code, 6–7
    copying and pasting, 12
    catch block, 13
    code improvement, 17
    code, future tests, 16
    coding standards, 8–9

Scripting (*cont.*)
  debugging, 15–16
  declare and initialize
      variables, 18–19
  errors, 13
  forced exit, timeout, 5
  hardcoded coordinates, 10
  language, GUI Tests, 17–18
  leaving, codes, 17
  operations, 10
  options, logical conditions, 8
  pauses, 3–4
  record and play functionality, 1–2
  running (*see* Running scripts)
  separate code, data, 14
  standard libraries, 11–12
  static code analyzers, 9
  try block, 13
Static code analyzers, 9

■ **T, U**

Testing
  automation, 26
  calculations and outputs, 21

cloud services (*see* Cloud testing)
correct approach, 21
CRUD functionality, 22
developers, 24–25
error and warning, 27
failure, 22
functional tests, 21
incorrect, 21
manual, 23–24
methodologies
    automation tools, companies, 28
    disadvantages, 28
    Keyword-Driven, 28
    misuse, 27
    pilot project, 29
    verification, individual bugs, 28
record creation, edition and
    deletion, 22–23
run tests (*see* Running scripts)
source data, 22
Windows calculator, 22

■ **V, W, X, Y, Z**

Verification, screenshots, 41

Get the eBook for only $5!

Why limit yourself?

With most of our titles available in both PDF and ePUB format, you can access your content wherever and however you wish—on your PC, phone, tablet, or reader.

Since you've purchased this print book, we are happy to offer you the eBook for just $5.

To learn more, go to http://www.apress.com/companion or contact support@apress.com.

Apress®

Printed in the United States
By Bookmasters